THE IMPOSTER

UNMASKING THE ABSALOM SPIRIT

BY

DAVE WILLIAMS

THE IMPOSTER
UNMASKING THE ABSALOM SPIRIT

All rights reserved. No part of this publication may be reproduced, stored in a retrieval system, or transmitted in any form or by any means—electronic, mechanical, photocopy, recording, or any other—except for brief quotations in printed reviews, without prior permission of the publisher.

Unless otherwise noted, all Scripture quotations are taken from the *King James Version* of the Bible.

Scripture quotations marked (AMP) are taken from the *Amplified Bible*, copyright © 1954, 1958, 1962, 1964, 1965, 1987 by The Lockman Foundation. Used by permission. (www.Lockman.org)

Scripture quotations marked (MSG) are taken from *The Message*, copyright © 1993, 1994, 1995, 1996, 2000, 2001, 2002. Used by permission of NavPress Publishing Group.

Scripture quotations marked (NKJV) are taken from the *New King James Version*, copyright © 1982 by Thomas Nelson, Inc. Used by permission. All rights reserved.

Scripture quotations marked (NLT) are taken from the *Holy Bible, New Living Translation*, copyright © 1996, 2004. Used by permission of Tyndale House Publishers, Inc., Wheaton, Illinois 60189. All rights reserved.

Copyright © 2010 by Dr. David R. Williams

ISBN 978-0-938020-95-0

First Printed 2010

Cover Design by Timothy Henley

Printed in the United States of America

OTHER BOOKS BY DAVE WILLIAMS

ABC's Of Success And Happiness
Angels: They Are Watching You
Beatitudes: Success 101
The Beauty Of Holiness
Coming Into The Wealthy Place
The Desires Of Your Heart
Developing The Spirit Of A Conqueror
Elite Prayer Warriors
Emerging Leaders
End-Times Bible Prophecy
Faith Goals
Filled
Genuine Prosperity
Gifts That Shape Your Life And Change Your World
Have You Heard From The Lord Lately?
How To Be A High Performance Believer
How To Help Your Pastor Succeed
The Jezebel Spirit
Miracle Breakthrough Power Of The First Fruit
Miracle Results Of Fasting
The New Life...The Start Of Something Wonderful
Pacesetting Leadership
The Pastor's Minute
The Presence Of God
Private Garden
Radical Fasting
Radical Forgiveness
Radical Healing
Regaining Your Spiritual Momentum
The Road To Radical Riches
Seven Sign Posts On The Road To Spiritual Maturity
Skill for Battle: The Art of Spiritual Warfare
Somebody Out There Needs You
Toxic Committees & Venomous Boards
What To Do If You Miss The Rapture
The World Beyond
Your Pastor: A Key To Your Personal Wealth

CONTENTS

1. The Malignant Impostor.................... 7
2. Frustrated With Life.................... 11
3. Repeating Lucifer's Sin.................... 17
4. Exposing The Politician.................... 23
5. Stealing Hearts.................... 29
6. Payday.................... 35
7. How Can This Happen?.................... 39
8. Standing Up To The Impostor.................... 45
9. Personal "Bewares!".................... 53
10. The Preeminence of Jesus Christ.................... 57

The Absalom spirit has brought more hell to earth than anyone can imagine.

CHAPTER 1

THE MALIGNANT IMPOSTOR

The story of Absalom is not a pretty one. It wasn't pretty in King David's day, and it isn't pretty today.

The Absalom spirit has brought more hell to earth than anyone can imagine. This spirit is charming, deceptive, cunning, subtle, and treacherous. This spirit brings chaos and confusion to a church or business—all under the pretense of genuine concern.

The Mount Hope Church Bible Training Institute has hundreds of graduates from the School of Ministry Training. Hundreds of pastors from various denominations have attended our ministry school in Lansing, Michigan, or our annual Church Planter's School in St. Pete Beach, Florida. We currently have 216 credentialed ministers in our own Mount Hope Church network.

I've heard firsthand the heartbreaking stories of the effects of the modern-day Absalom spirit.

I have met with Methodist, Baptist, Church of God, Assemblies of God, Word of Faith, Independent, Nazarene, Presbyterian, and Lutheran ministers in their times of crisis, and—by far—the greatest confusion, chaos, ministry pain, and discouragement comes when these sincere pastors come face-to-face with an Absalom spirit.

I've ministered to countless pastors and businesspeople alike who have struggled to understand, "What's going on here?" when they are facing an Absalom-like personality.

How many decent and loving people have been destroyed by the insincerity of Absalom's "care" and "concern" for the church, the district, or the business? Like Absalom, Adolph Hitler's rise to fame, and ultimate control of Germany, initially appeared to be motivated by concern and the intention of doing good.

The spirit of Absalom is a personification of a malignant usurper—an impostor.

Absalom ended up bringing shame to his father, his family, and his kingdom.

In this small book, we'll look at the biblical Absalom, whom I'll typically refer to as "Absalom" or "the original Absalom." In referring to a modern day Absalom, I'll call it the "Absalom personality," or the "Absalom spirit."

The Original Absalom

Let's take a look at the sad story of the original Absalom and see what we can learn about how this spirit operates today. The name Absalom denotes disobedience, pridefulness, hypocrisy, self-promotion, and rebellion.

Absalom, the third son of King David, had a lot going for him. He was strikingly handsome from head to toe—physically flawless. He could have been a super model. His physical appearance was stunning.

> Now in all Israel there was no one who was praised as much as Absalom for his good looks. From the sole of his foot to the crown of his head there was no blemish in him.
> —2 Samuel 14:25 (NKJV)

But Absalom was frustrated and angry. Let's take a look at Absalom's situation and how he chose to handle it.

An *Absalom spirit thrives on hidden agendas, concealed strategies, and secret alliances.*

CHAPTER 2

FRUSTRATED WITH LIFE

Absalom was frustrated with life, and this is typical of modern-day Absaloms. They seem to burn with an inner anger. They are frustrated with life, their ministry, or their perceived station in life. They often search for value in personal pursuits rather than in God himself, and thus become like the man Solomon described:

> Throughout their lives, they live under a cloud—frustrated, discouraged, and angry.
> —Ecclesiastes 5:17 (NLT)

They frequently imagine they deserve more recognition than their achievements merit. In fact, the original Absalom built himself a monument, the same as many evil dictators have done.

> Now Absalom in his lifetime had reared up for himself a pillar which is in the King's Valley....

> He called the pillar after his own name, and to this day it is called Absalom's Monument.
> —2 Samuel 18:18 (AMP)

Absalom was bitter and upset. Years before, Absalom took offense with his brother Amnon, the way some believers get offended with others today. He felt qualified to sit in judgment of Amnon and even determined his punishment. He plotted and carried out his brother's murder. Because of this crime, he was held under "house arrest" by order of his father, King David. Absalom was unrepentant for his actions and felt wronged.

False Criteria

Absalom had a way of judging everything by his own criteria. His brother Amnon sinned. Absalom determined he deserved to die, so he arranged for Amnon's execution. King David would never have approved of Absalom's judgment of Amnon, so Absalom plotted it all on his own. Instead of seeing himself as a murderer, he saw himself as a hero, worthy of a Medal of Honor or some other special recognition for his "honorable" achievement. His thinking was twisted.

In the same manner, a modern Absalom will get offended with leadership then—secretly—arrange the subtle "execution" of the leader's reputation, achievements, or integrity. Just as Absalom did in reaction to his brothers offense, an Absalom spirit typically harbors camouflaged bitterness, unresolved offenses, disappointments, and anger.

When a modern-day Absalom's ideas are not accepted by the leadership, he becomes offended. Once a person takes on an offense and does not resolve it, he becomes offended at almost everything—no matter how minor. He will carry that unresolved offense in his heart, often searching for others to agree with him in the offense (2 Samuel 13:20–29).

Hidden Agenda

An Absalom spirit thrives on hidden agendas, concealed strategies, and secret alliances.

Absalom believes:

- Authority cannot to be trusted
- Authority is incompetent
- "I know the right way to handle this."

A modern-day Absalom harbors hidden contempt, hidden hatred of authority, and concealed plans of revenge against authority and any others who are submitted to that authority. The Absalom personality will carry his offenses to as many individuals as possible, spreading discontent through a variety of means (2 Samuel 13:22).

Hidden Rebellion

An Absalom spirit is rebellious, and that rebellion increasingly grows like a cancer. At some point, that cancer can become lethal if not dealt with firmly (2 Samuel 14:27–30).

> For rebellion is as the sin of witchcraft, and stubbornness is as iniquity and idolatry. Because thou hast rejected the word of the LORD, he hath also rejected thee from being king.
> —1 Samuel 15:23

When an Absalom spirit is at work in a church or business, you will notice turmoil and confusion, and you will probably experience a churning stomach and chaotic thought life. This is because the sin of rebellion seems to release spirits of witchcraft. I'm not talking about the kind of witchcraft that is a work of the flesh (Galatians 5:19–21) but the kind where demons are loosed on an entire group or family because of the spirit of rebellion.

St. Paul spoke of this rebellious spirit becoming more dominant as we approach Jesus' return.

> For the mystery of lawlessness (that hidden principle of rebellion against constituted authority) is already at work in the world.…
> —2 Thessalonians 2:7a (AMP)

Jesus himself spoke of the escalating conditions as we approach the "Day of the Lord."

> "A brother will betray his brother to death, a father will betray his own child, and children will rebel against their parents and cause them to be killed."
> —Matthew 10:21 (NLT)

Is the malignant impostor—the Absalom spirit—simply following Lucifer's example?

CHAPTER 3

REPEATING LUCIFER'S SIN

An Absalom personality works subtly to marginalize the true leader. In time, he maneuvers to demonize the leader and betray him by destroying his influence among as many followers as possible. Doesn't this sound eerily similar to Lucifer's betrayal of God and his capture of the hearts of one-third of the angelic host?

The end result of participating in rebellion and betrayal is always the same. Whether the name is Korah, Dathan, Abiram, Haman, Jezebel, Ahithophel, or Judas the story never changes. Rebellion *never* leads to a happy ending.

Desire To Be In Command

An Absalom personality thinks he is in competition with the leadership and regularly distorts and misrepresents the decisions or directives the leader gives.

The Absalom spirit possesses a desire to be in authority but is not motivated by purity or a desire to do God's will, although he puts on a good show.

Now that we know a little bit about Absalom, let's get to the heart of the Absalom personality (or spirit). You can study the history of this entire matter in 2 Samuel, chapters 13–18. The purpose of this book is not to delve deeply into the matters of the historic Absalom, but to highlight his tactics to help you identify the contemporary Absalom spirit at work and deal with it successfully.

Absalom's Tactics

Let's see what we can learn from the tactics of the original Absalom. Here's an overview of the events and motivations found in 2 Samuel 15:1–12:

An Absalom spirit works at impressing and stealing the hearts of the people who are under authority. His goal is to eventually "dethrone" and replace the one in authority.

> ***"Pious persons are glad to see others appear religious, and this gives occasion for deceptions. The policy of wicked men, and the subtlety of Satan, are exerted to draw good persons to countenance base designs."*** [1]

Absalom is a self-promoter seeking the praise of men.

---

[1] Matthew Henry, ***Concise Bible Commentary***, ***Volume II, 2 Samuel***, Public Domain.

After this, Absalom bought a chariot and horses, and he hired fifty bodyguards to run ahead of him.

—2 Samuel 15:1 (NLT)

Absalom maintains a ***carefully orchestrated and meticulously projected image*** designed to impress. As people recognize and praise him, he begins to believe that he is more spiritual or wiser than the true leader.

> [2] He got up early every morning and went out to the gate of the city. When people brought a case to the king for judgment, Absalom would ask where in Israel they were from, and they would tell him their tribe.
>
> [3] Then Absalom would say, "You've really got a strong case here! It's too bad the king doesn't have anyone to hear it.
>
> [4] "I wish I were the judge. Then everyone could bring their cases to me for judgment, and I would give them justice!"
>
> [5] When people tried to bow before him, Absalom wouldn't let them. Instead, he took them by the hand and kissed them.
>
> [6] Absalom did this with everyone who came to the king for judgment, and so he stole the hearts of all the people of Israel.
>
> —2 Samuel 15:2–6 (NLT)

Master Manipulator

The Absalom personality is a master of manipulation. He assures people, "You are special to me." "You are my friend." "I love you more than the pastor loves you. I will spend quality time with you. He doesn't." "I'm telling you this because I really trust you."

An Absalom spirit is displayed in selfish ambition—disguised to appear as service to others, to the church, district, or business (2 Samuel 15:2).

The modern-day Absalom seeks opportunities for self-advancement at the expense of others. He will attack the decisions of the leaders and infer they are incompetent.

Sadly, with this critical spirit, the Absalom personality can no longer receive any spiritual food or direction from the leadership. Nothing the pastor/leader does is good enough for Absalom. Even if Absalom's ideas are implemented, it's never good enough. This personality always finds some fault (2 Samuel 15:3).

An Absalom spirit is revealed in divisiveness, antagonism, and negative criticism of authority. He actively seeks out leadership-type individuals that will seemingly approve of his actions (2 Samuel 5:3).

Absalom feeds his followers with his faultfinding and critical spirit. Minor things, usually not related to God's spiritual qualifications, will be made major issues, such as what kind of car the pastor drives, his salary, his style of leadership, or his approach to challenges (2 Samuel 15:4).

An Absalom spirit exhibits false humility (2 Samuel 15:5).

Not only is the Absalom personality a master manipulator, he is also a master politician.

The Absalom personality sees matters from only a human point of view rather than God's.

CHAPTER 4

EXPOSING THE POLITICIAN

The original Absalom was a master politician: backslapping, hand kissing, and complimenting. His victims did not discern his real motivation and the trap he was planning to spring on them. Jesus said:

> "…Hypocrites! For you cross land and sea to make one convert, and then you turn that person into twice the child of hell you yourselves are!"
> —Matthew 23:15b (NLT)

You know the scenario. You've probably experienced it yourself. Someone calls to arrange a lunch appointment with you. He implies that it's rather urgent that he meet with you. He may be a person you respected in the past. He may be a pastor leading what appears to be a good church, or he may be a businessman. He may even be some kind of elected official in your denomination. You have no reason to doubt his sincerity or integrity, so you schedule the meeting and sit down for lunch.

You pray over your food and chat. He does most of the talking. He tells you how he's being honored, where he's preaching, and how he has obtained favor with some well-known people. Names are dropped—names he believes you respect. He then showers you with an array of compliments for your service to God's Kingdom and tells you what a great asset you are to the church or district or business. You appreciate his kind words of adulation and commendation. Who wouldn't love to hear those kinds of things?

After awhile, the tone of the lunch meeting gradually changes. "Trial balloons" start going up to see where you stand on certain matters and issues. While you are still feeling good about all the flattering comments, he begins pointing out problems, criticizing leadership, and making subtle, degrading remarks about someone in authority. His subtle slander is a carefully crafted design to come across in a "holy" way. He's only telling you this because he trusts you and because he's "deeply concerned" about the leadership or direction of the church (ministry, denomination, district, business—you name it).

If you are discerning, you begin to get the distinct impression that this is more than a friendly lunch appointment. He never says it, but you get the feeling he is campaigning for a change in leadership—and offering himself as the candidate.

If you're like me, you begin to berate yourself for thinking such a negative thing about this fine Christian man. But you can't seem to shake some of the thoughts he planted.

You pray for God's inner peace, but it's difficult to dismiss some of the issues he presented to you. These seeds keep swirling around in your mind, trying to take root.

Could it be that he traveled to you ("crossing land and sea") to make you his convert? Could it be that, like Absalom, he's trying to turn you into twice the child of hell he is? Oh, he doesn't see himself as a child of hell. He sees himself as a hero, a leader, and a force for change.

> "What sorrow awaits you teachers of religious law and you Pharisees. Hypocrites! For you cross land and sea to make one convert, and then you turn that person into twice the child of hell you yourselves are!"
> —Matthew 23:15 (NLT)

Suspicious Behavior

Observe him in the months that follow. Here's what you'll typically find: He will subtly and stealthily continue to point out flaws in the leadership of the church, business, or denomination. He will work to create distractions for the true leader in order to prevent positive achievements that could be credited to the leader. Gradually, there will be more and more openness about his discontent—all under the guise of his "concern."

Start observing the people with whom he surrounds himself. You'll discover, as I have, that his closest associates all seem to be walking in some kind of offense themselves. They have little respect for authority. You'll notice they see themselves as important leaders, all the while continuing their faultfinding, criticism, and complaining, and obstructing progress for the God-appointed leader. And each of them will be acting as mini-campaign managers for the Absalom personality.

I pray the proverbial "light" will dawn on you before you get infected with the Absalom spirit. This man is trying to steal hearts so he can get into a position that belongs to another man.

To offer an Absalom spirit any support at all is to debase your own soul, bringing it eventually to the point of decay.

The Absalom spirit is to the soul what AIDS is to the body.

This scenario has played over and over again in churches, districts, denominations and businesses. Different names, different locations, and different twists, but the same spirit—Absalom!

The Absalom personality sees matters from only a human point of view rather than God's. "How can I influence this person?" "How many votes do I need to win?"

One of Satan's greatest tactics is to get believer's eyes off God's purposes and on to human maneuvering. In fact, Jesus rebuked Peter for this very thing.

> Jesus turned to Peter and said, "Get away from me, Satan! You are a dangerous trap to me. You are seeing things merely from a human point of view, not from God's."
> —Matthew 16:23 (NLT)

Are you willing to have your heart stolen by an impostor?

An *Absalom spirit employs subtle seduction.*

CHAPTER

STEALING HEARTS

> The thief cometh not, but for to steal, and to kill, and to destroy: I am come that they might have life, and that they might have it more abundantly.
> —John 10:10

An Absalom spirit is a thief, **stealing the hearts and loyalty of the people away from their true authority**. When the Absalom personality feels that many are following him, he gradually brings his disloyalty out into the open. Now the people are forced to make a choice between the genuine leader and the Absalom who has deceived them (2 Samuel 15:6).

> ⁷ After four years, Absalom said to the king, "Let me go to Hebron to offer a sacrifice to the LORD and fulfill a vow I made to him.
> ⁸ For while your servant was at Geshur in Aram, I promised to sacrifice to the LORD in Hebron if he would bring me back to Jerusalem."

⁹ "All right," the king told him. "Go and fulfill your vow." So Absalom went to Hebron.
¹⁰ But while he was there, he sent secret messengers to all the tribes of Israel to stir up a rebellion against the king. "As soon as you hear the ram's horn," his message read, "you are to say, 'Absalom has been crowned king in Hebron.'"
—2 Samuel 15:7–10 (NLT)

Making His Move

After four years of criticizing and secretly undermining the king and building himself up in the eyes of the people, Absalom was ready to make his move. His plan was to make his debut as king where David did, and where he was born, Hebron.

Now the awful truth emerges. People must make a choice between their leader and the Absalom who has deceived them all by his duplicity. Usually the Absalom spirit does not ultimately deceive the majority, but he has caused enough division to foster doubt in the remainder of the followers.

Absalom's Conspiracy

Absalom is dangerous. The Absalom spirit justifies his conspiracy to everyone by focusing attention on all the minor issues he has found fault with in the leadership. Usually the Absalom personality does not have legitimate accusations, such as the preaching of false doctrines or blatant sin on the part of the leader.

An Absalom spirit employs subtle seduction. Absalom doesn't necessarily need a large group to implement his move; even a small band of followers, three or four in key positions, will be sufficient. He knows he has stolen their hearts (2 Samuel 15:11-13).

The Great Pretender

A sense of uneasiness now descends over the people.

> *"The story tells very vividly how he adopted the familiar tactics of pretenders."* [1]

> [11] He took 200 men from Jerusalem with him as guests, but they knew nothing of his intentions.
> [12] While Absalom was offering the sacrifices, he sent for Ahithophel, one of David's counselors who lived in Giloh. Soon many others also joined Absalom, and the conspiracy gained momentum.
> —2 Samuel 15:11–12 (NLT)

An Absalom personality is not only a liar, but a religious hypocrite too (2 Samuel 15:12). You'll notice while Absalom was offering the sacrifices publicly, he was carrying out his plot to take over authority in secret.

Jesus constantly confronted the religious hypocrites. These pretenders didn't fool him, and they

---

[1] Alexander McClaren, 2 Samuel 15:1–12 *Pardoned Sin Punished, Sermons on 2 Samuel*, Public Domain

shouldn't fool any born-again, Spirit-filled person who is walking in the Spirit and staying true to God's Word.

> But Jesus perceived their wickedness, and said, Why tempt ye me, ye hypocrites?
> —Matthew 22:18

It's enlightening to see that Jesus equated hypocrisy with wickedness. The religious pretense of the Absalom personality often deceives undiscerning Christians.

> $^{13–15}$ They're a sorry bunch—pseudo-apostles, lying preachers, crooked workers—posing as Christ's agents but sham to the core. And no wonder! Satan does it all the time, dressing up as a beautiful angel of light. So it shouldn't surprise us when his servants masquerade as servants of God. But they're not getting by with anything. They'll pay for it in the end.
> —2 Corinthians 11:13–15 (MSG)

And, oh, what a payday is ahead for the Absalom personality and his victims.

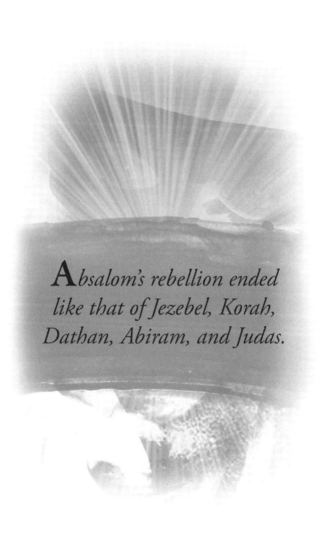

Absalom's rebellion ended like that of Jezebel, Korah, Dathan, Abiram, and Judas.

CHAPTER 6

PAYDAY

The Judgment That Surely Follows

There is a Biblical principle that states: If the root is evil, then the fruit will also be evil. This means, then, that a group birthed from the workings of an Absalom spirit will suffer the same fate in due time.

> For if the firstfruit be holy, the lump is also holy: and if the root be holy, so are the branches.
> —Romans 11:16

> The soul that sinneth, it shall die. The son shall not bear the iniquity of the father, neither shall the father bear the iniquity of the son: the righteousness of the righteous shall be upon him, and the wickedness of the wicked shall be upon him.
> —Ezekiel 18:20

"The soul that sinneth, it shall die." Absalom must have known this truth, but ignored it. There is always a payday.

> I will turn against such people and make a terrible example of them, eliminating them from among my people. Then you will know that I am the Lord.
>
> —Ezekiel 14:8 (NLT)

Absalom **died in a most revealing way**. His head got caught in a tree and he was left dangling until he was executed. Caught by his head! In biblical typology, the head stands for authority and leadership.

Absalom set himself up as head, and by his head he was judged!

> 9–10 Absalom ran into David's men, but was out in front of them riding his mule, when the mule ran under the branches of a huge oak tree. Absalom's head was caught in the oak and he was left dangling between heaven and earth, the mule running right out from under him. A solitary soldier saw him and reported it to Joab, "I just saw Absalom hanging from an oak tree!"
>
> 14–15 Joab said, "I can't waste my time with you." He then grabbed three knives and stabbed Absalom in the heart while he was still alive in the tree; by then Absalom was surrounded by ten of Joab's armor bearers; they hacked away at him and killed him.
>
> —2 Samuel 18: 9–10, 14–15 (MSG)

They "hacked away at him." What an awful way to die! He hacked away at the authority of Israel's anointed leader, and now it was payday. His own life was hacked away.

Absalom's Downfall

Absalom's rebellion ended like that of Jezebel, Korah, Dathan, Abiram, and Judas. They fell through pride, and their lives ended prematurely and tragically.

It is dangerous ground to sow strife and cause division in the body of Christ. The Lord hates the sowing of discord among brethren.

> [16] These six things doth the LORD hate: yea, seven are an abomination unto him:
> [17] A proud look, a lying tongue, and hands that shed innocent blood,
> [18] An heart that deviseth wicked imaginations, feet that be swift in running to mischief,
> [19] A false witness that speaketh lies, and he that soweth discord among brethren.
> —Proverbs 6:16–19

> So anyone who rebels against authority is rebelling against what God has instituted, and they will be punished.
> —Romans 13:2 (NLT)

How can a genuine believer be taken over by an Absalom spirit?

> [9] I wrote unto the church: but Diotrephes, who loveth to have the preeminence among them, receiveth us not.
> [10] Wherefore, if I come, I will remember his deeds which he doeth, prating against us with malicious words: and not content therewith, neither doth he himself receive the brethren, and forbiddeth them that would, and casteth them out of the church.
> —3 John 1:9–10

Those who have the responsibility of leadership are easy targets for an Absalom spirit. Stay loyal to the leader who trusts you, even though he or she may not be perfect.

Be loyal or begone.

Concluding Words

Remember these words of King David, Absalom's father:

> [4] I will reject perverse ideas and stay away from every evil.
> [5] I will not tolerate people who slander their neighbors. I will not endure conceit and pride.
> [6] I will search for faithful people to be my companions. Only those who are above reproach will be allowed to serve me.
> [7] I will not allow deceivers to serve in my house, and liars will not stay in my presence.
> [8] My daily task will be to ferret out the wicked and free the city of the LORD from their grip.
> —Psalm 101:4–8 (NLT)

Absalom's Downfall

Absalom's rebellion ended like that of Jezebel, Korah, Dathan, Abiram, and Judas. They fell through pride, and their lives ended prematurely and tragically.

It is dangerous ground to sow strife and cause division in the body of Christ. The Lord hates the sowing of discord among brethren.

> [16] These six things doth the LORD hate: yea, seven are an abomination unto him:
> [17] A proud look, a lying tongue, and hands that shed innocent blood,
> [18] An heart that deviseth wicked imaginations, feet that be swift in running to mischief,
> [19] A false witness that speaketh lies, and he that soweth discord among brethren.
> —Proverbs 6:16–19

> So anyone who rebels against authority is rebelling against what God has instituted, and they will be punished.
> —Romans 13:2 (NLT)

How can a genuine believer be taken over by an Absalom spirit?

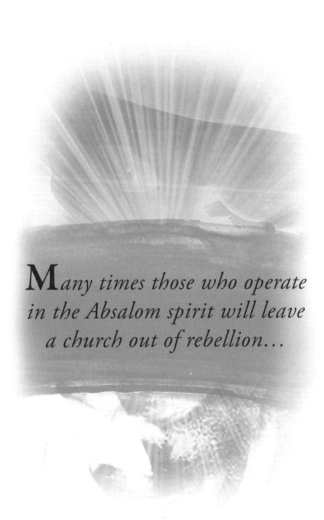

Many times those who operate in the Absalom spirit will leave a church out of rebellion...

CHAPTER 7

HOW CAN THIS HAPPEN?

What Caused Absalom's Treacherous Sin?

Unresolved offenses, selfish ambition, and hatred led to Absalom's unforgiving attitude and bitterness. His motivations were never pure. His aim was revenge, to discredit and ruin established authority. Unresolved offenses always lead to hatred and betrayal.

> [3] And as he sat upon the mount of Olives, the disciples came unto him privately, saying, Tell us, when shall these things be? and what shall be the sign of thy coming, and of the end of the world?
> [10] And then shall many be offended, and shall betray one another, and shall hate one another.
> —Matthew 24:3 &10

Why Is This Spirit So Hard To Handle?

This spirit is difficult to deal with because people are emotionally attached to Absalom personalities through relationships. Absalom personalities are nice, usually friendly, lovable, and popular. Everyone loved Absalom—even David. Dealing with them makes leaders appear unloving or judgmental.

Prepare for a Personal Attack!

When you try to help a person infected by the Absalom spirit to see his guilt, prepare to be attacked. Or, when you show support for the true leader, you will be attacked in some way by the Absalom personality, most likely through his underlings and devotees.

Being a religious hypocrite, like the Pharisees who arranged the execution of Jesus, the Absalom personality will work hard to discredit you. Unfortunately, the only way to deal with him is to cut him off.

Had David not allowed Absalom back into the kingdom, he would not have experienced betrayal and temporary loss of the kingdom.

Many times those who operate in the Absalom spirit will leave a church out of rebellion, but want to stay in fellowship a bit. "We are still a part of the Kingdom of God even if we are not in the same fellowship" is their reasoning. The logic sounds good, but the fact that they are causing division indicates their true motive is ***not*** fellowship.

> *One thing the Absalom spirit cannot fail to do is to speak against what he's left behind.* [1]

Absalom Characteristics in a Nutshell

- They seek an audience.
- Kindness and favor are their tools. Sometimes they give special gifts and pour out exaggerated "sweetness." Absalom caused division by sweetness, "stealing the hearts of David's followers."
- The Absalom spirit tells people, "You are special to me." This is a pernicious characteristic of deception; you don't know you are being deceived and set up. This is why discernment is critically important.
- Special treatment: fellowship, trips, gifts, or favors. Everyone likes to be treated in a special way. Everyone wants to feel special. But when it's an Absalom personality making the offer, you must see it as bait, and run the other way.
- Nothing the pastor/leader does is good enough for Absalom. Behind the scenes they covertly plant doubt concerning

---

[1] Peter McArthur, *The Issachar Ministry, Identifying the Absalom Spirit*, www.issacharministry.org

leadership. They look for faults in pastors and leaders.
- They have a hidden agenda. Absalom's motives were not known until they manifested, and then it was too late. You know where you stand with a Jezebel spirit or Korah personality, but Absalom is sneaky and works behind your back.
- Absalom tells you the things you want to hear. A pastor's job is to speak the truth in love. Sometimes that truth hurts and calls for change, but it is always for our good.
- An Absalom spirit eventually comes forward with open disloyalty and division.
- Absalom's goal is to use his power and position to advance his own agenda, not to help you reach your goals and dreams.
- Absalom appears to be affectionate—out of selfish motivation for personal gain. You will never be led into a closer relationship with Jesus by associating with an Absalom spirit.
- Absalom is self-seeking and egotistical and loves to listen to complaints that help to undermine authority.
- Absalom's sole purpose is to manipulate so he can get something that God hasn't given him!

> They speak vanity every one with his neighbour: with flattering lips and with a double heart do they speak.
>
> —Psalm 12:2

- Absalom enlisted others to his cause, following the pattern of Lucifer. He sought out the advice of Ahithophel (Bathsheba's grandfather). The Absalom spirit also looks to someone with a fatherly nature to support him—someone he feels others respect. He may "drop" the names of those he wants you to believe support him.
- The Absalom spirit isn't ashamed to "drop names" of people he knows and deems to be prominent or powerful in order to convince others that these people agree with him.
- Discontented people will enlist others in Absalom's cause, rallying their own troops for rebellion.
- Absalom personalities create division to benefit their own vengeance or cause.
- Absalom spirits do their best to sow seeds of discontent with the purpose of undermining the authority God has approved and appointed.

It's time to take a stand against anything and anyone preventing Jesus from having preeminence.

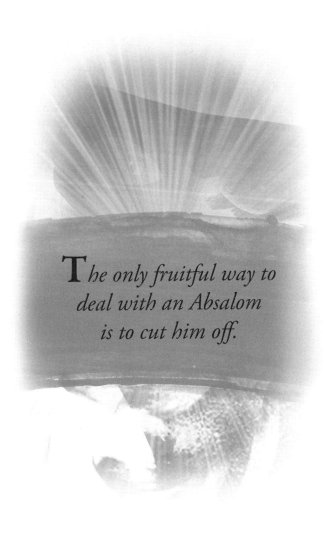

STANDING UP TO THE IMPOSTOR

How to Deal with The Absalom Spirit:

1. *Leaders must exercise the gift of discerning of spirits* (1 Corinthians 12:10).

   A God-loyal person will see right through the wicked and undo the evil they've planned.
   —Proverbs 21:12 (MSG)

2. *Leaders must demonstrate proper role modeling.* If the rest of the sheep see you hobnobbing with Absalom, then they will think it is okay.

3. *Leaders must protect.* Protect the sheep from being kissed by Absalom. Wolves don't come dressed as wolves, but as sheep. Doing nothing guarantees that

Absalom will worm his way into the seat of authority.

> Beware of false prophets, which come to you in sheep's clothing, but inwardly they are ravening wolves.
> —Matthew 7:15

> ²⁸ "Now it's up to you. Be on your toes—both for yourselves and your congregation of sheep. The Holy Spirit has put you in charge of these people—God's people they are—to guard and protect them. God himself thought they were worth dying for.
> ²⁹⁻³¹ "I know that as soon as I'm gone, vicious wolves are going to show up and rip into this flock, men from your very own ranks twisting words so as to seduce disciples into following them instead of Jesus. So stay awake and keep up your guard. Remember those three years I kept at it with you, never letting up, pouring my heart out with you, one after another."
> —Acts 20:28–31 (MSG)

> After careful scrutiny, a wise leader makes a clean sweep of rebels and dolts.
> —Proverbs 20:26 (MSG)

4. ***Stop tolerating their antics.*** Put an end to the Absalom spirit. Remember, this is a demonic spirit you are dealing with. Their involvement comes against God's established authority and seeks to divide His kingdom. Nehemiah, for example, refused to give in to the antics of the Absalom personalities trying to distract him.

STANDING UP TO THE IMPOSTER

¹⁻² When Sanballat, Tobiah, Geshem the Arab, and the rest of our enemies heard that I had rebuilt the wall and that there were no more breaks in it—even though I hadn't yet installed the gates—Sanballat and Geshem sent this message: "Come and meet with us at Kephirim in the valley of Ono."

²⁻³ I knew they were scheming to hurt me so I sent messengers back with this: "I'm doing a great work; I can't come down. Why should the work come to a standstill just so I can come down to see you?"

⁴ Four times they sent this message and four times I gave them my answer.

⁵⁻⁶ The fifth time—same messenger, same message—Sanballat sent an unsealed letter with this message:

⁶⁻⁷ "The word is out among the nations—and Geshem says it's true—that you and the Jews are planning to rebel. That's why you are rebuilding the wall. The word is that you want to be king and that you have appointed prophets to announce in Jerusalem, 'There's a king in Judah!' The king is going to be told all this—don't you think we should sit down and have a talk?"

⁸ I sent him back this: "There's nothing to what you're saying. You've made it all up."

⁹ They were trying to intimidate us into quitting. They thought, "They'll give up; they'll never finish it." I prayed, "Give me strength."

—Nehemiah 6:1–9 (MSG)

The Absalom spirit is strengthened if it appears the pastor or leader is paranoid or weak.

5. ***Don't give them a place in the life of your ministry or business.*** The only

fruitful way to deal with an Absalom is to cut him off.

And have no fellowship with the unfruitful works of darkness, but rather reprove them.
—Ephesians 5:11

So humble yourselves before God. Resist the devil, and he will flee from you.
—James 4:7 (NLT)

6. *Avoid promoting people until their true character is proven*, and never put someone with Absalom characteristics in any place of leadership or authority.

[1] Sin whispers to the wicked, deep within their hearts. They have no fear of God at all.
[2] In their blind conceit, they cannot see how wicked they really are.
[3] Everything they say is crooked and deceitful. They refuse to act wisely or do good.
[4] They lie awake at night, hatching sinful plots. Their actions are never good. They make no attempt to turn from evil.
—Psalm 36:1–4 (NLT)

7. *Be on guard and mark those who cause division and avoid them.*

[17] I appeal to you, brethren, to be on your guard concerning those who create dissensions and difficulties and cause divisions, in opposition to the doctrine (the teaching) which you have been taught. [I warn you to turn aside from them, to] avoid them.
[18] For such persons do not serve our Lord Christ but their own appetites and base desires,

and by ingratiating and flattering speech, they beguile the hearts of the unsuspecting and simpleminded [people].

—Romans 16:17–18 (AMP)

8. *Pray for them.* Set up intercessors you trust to hold special times of prayer. I believe, through our prayers, many will be delivered from these spirits and be fruitful once again in God's kingdom.

[26] Woe to you, when all men shall speak well of you! for so did their fathers to the false prophets.
[27] But I say unto you which hear, Love your enemies, do good to them which hate you,
[28] Bless them that curse you, and pray for them which despitefully use you.

—Luke 6:26–28

9. *Realize that eventually their own pride will bring them down.*

[9] And Absalom met the servants of David. And Absalom rode upon a mule, and the mule went under the thick boughs of a great oak, and his head caught hold of the oak, and he was taken up between the heaven and the earth; and the mule that was under him went away.
[14] Then said Joab, I may not tarry thus with thee. And he took three darts in his hand, and thrust them through the heart of Absalom, while he was yet alive in the midst of the oak.

—2 Samuel 18:9 & 14

Pride goes before destruction, and a haughty spirit before a fall.

—Proverbs 16:18

In the next chapter, we'll look at some important cautions that will provide you with a vaccination against the Absalom virus.

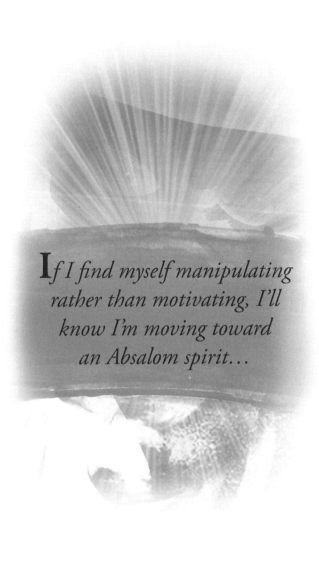

CHAPTER 9

PERSONAL "BEWARES!"

Personal Cautions:

- If I ever am more concerned about my recognition than the mission, then malevolent, degenerative forces are at work!
- If I ever seek to manipulate someone for personal gain, I have sided with Satan against God's anointing!
- If I ever dig a pit for someone else, I am sure to be buried in that very grave!
- If I ever believe that I need what someone else has to be happy, whether it's possessions or positions, I have lost sight of God, lost my security in him, and have taken a step closer to operating in the Absalom spirit.

- If I ever am not content with what I have, I can be sure I won't be content if I get what I want.
- If I ever sow seeds of dissension and division (and diminish spiritual authority), I can be sure that I am operating in the spirit of Lucifer and not the attitude of the Christ of Calvary! [1]
- If I ever think, "If I were in charge," it's a sure sign I do not have what it takes to *be* in charge.
- If I ever believe myself to be more in "touch" with people and issues than the leadership, I need to be humbled.
- If I ever find myself manipulating rather than motivating, I'll know I'm moving toward an Absalom spirit and must repent quickly.
- If I ever surround myself with people who have unresolved offenses, I'll know I'm on the road to shame.
- If I ever find myself looking for ways to prove how much more I know or how much more gifted I am than the pastor or leader; I'll know Satan has stolen a piece of my soul.

---

[1] Bill Kirk, *The Absalom Spirit (The Causes and Cure of Satan's Deceitful Scheme)* 2 Samuel 15:1–5; James 3:14–43, http://isite71734.web03.intellisite.com/files/BK's Messages/ The Absalom Spirit.

- If I ever verbalize any agreement with disgruntled members, I'm unworthy to be a leader and I am debasing my own soul.
- If I ever find myself subtly criticizing my pastor or my leader, and I haven't sincerely invested time in praying for them, I can be sure that I am out of spiritual alignment and must either repent or prepare to sabotage my own future.
- If Jesus Christ, God's Son, does not have first place in my life, I know I am not walking in the path of righteousness, and I'm in danger of falling into sin.

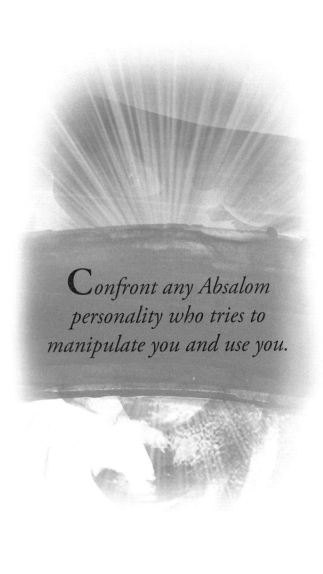

CHAPTER 10

THE PREEMINENCE OF JESUS CHRIST

Absalom Is Not Your Friend

When an Absalom spirit is active, Jesus no longer has preeminence. That's why there is confusion and chaos. The Absalom spirit, though praying hypocritically for show, does not want Jesus Christ to really enjoy preeminence. That's why this personality will call for committee meetings rather than genuine prayer meetings.

> And he is the head of the body, the church:
> who is the beginning, the firstborn from the dead;
> that in all things he might have the preeminence.
> —Colossians 1:18

St. John faced an Absalom personality in his day, and was not afraid to expose him and warn others of his treachery.

> [9] I wrote unto the church: but Diotrephes, who loveth to have the preeminence among them, receiveth us not.
> [10] Wherefore, if I come, I will remember his deeds which he doeth, prating against us with malicious words: and not content therewith, neither doth he himself receive the brethren, and forbiddeth them that would, and casteth them out of the church.
>
> —3 John 1:9–10

Those who have the responsibility of leadership are easy targets for an Absalom spirit. Stay loyal to the leader who trusts you, even though he or she may not be perfect.

Be loyal or begone.

Concluding Words

Remember these words of King David, Absalom's father:

> [4] I will reject perverse ideas and stay away from every evil.
> [5] I will not tolerate people who slander their neighbors. I will not endure conceit and pride.
> [6] I will search for faithful people to be my companions. Only those who are above reproach will be allowed to serve me.
> [7] I will not allow deceivers to serve in my house, and liars will not stay in my presence.
> [8] My daily task will be to ferret out the wicked and free the city of the LORD from their grip.
>
> —Psalm 101:4–8 (NLT)

THE PREEMINENCE OF JESUS CHRIST

> And he is the head of the body, the church:
> who is the beginning, the firstborn from the dead;
> that in all things he might have the preeminence.
> —Colossians 1.18

Confront any Absalom personality who tries to manipulate you and use you. Then go straight to your leader with a report concerning "Absalom" before it is too late.

Always seek God's Kingdom and his way of doing things (Matthew 6:33), and he will deliver you from the snares of the Absalom spirit. Then your life and ministry will be focused only on God's will and purpose so…

> …that in all things He [Jesus] might have the preeminence.
>
> —Colossians 1:18b

SELECTED BIBLIOGRAPHY

Ackroyd, Peter R., *The Second Book of Samuel*, Cambridge University Press, New York, 1977.

Anderson, A.A., *Word Biblical Commentary Vol. 11, 2 Samuel*, Thomas Nelson, Nashville, 1989.

Blank, Wayne, *Daily Bible Study*, at http://www.keyway.ca.

Britza, Ian M., *The Absalom Spirit: Revealing Disloyalty's Plan to Destroy You and Those you Trust*, Harrison House, Tulsa, 2004.

Cox, Paul, *The Absalom Spirit*, http://www.seventhundersministry.com.

Crazy Soul Winner weblog: *The Absalom Spirit*, posted 9/14/2007, http://www.xanga.com/crazysoulwinner.

Hertzberg, Hans W., *1 and 2 Samuel: A Commentary*, Westminster Press, Philadelphia, 1964.

Kirk, Bill, *The Absalom Spirit: The Causes and Cure of Satan's Deceitful Scheme*.

Ma'aseh de-Rabbi Joshua ben Levi, in Jellinek's *Betha-Midrash, ii., Jewish Encyclopedia*, 2002.

McArthur, Peter, *The Issachar Ministry*, eBooklet: http://issacharministry.org.au.

McCullough, Jackie, *Satisfaction of the Soul*, Destiny Image, Shippensburg, 2007.

Phillips, Mike & Marilyn, *Absalom: A Caution to Us All*, http://www.winonabethany.org/absalom.

Smith, H. P., *A Critical and Exegetical Commentary on the Books of Samuel*, T. and T. Clark, Edinburgh, 1904.

Testola, Dr. John, *Danger in the Local Church*, http://www.ecclesiaword.org.

Victory Life Church, *Discerning the Spirit of Absalom in the Church*, Folsom, CA.

Wesley, John, *John Wesley's Explanatory Notes, 2 Samuel*, Crosswalk.com.

About Dave Williams, D. Min.

Dr. Dave Williams is pastor of Mount Hope Church and International Outreach Ministries with headquarters in Lansing, Michigan. He has pastored there for almost 30 years, leading the church from 226 members to over 4,000 today.

The ministry campus comprises 60 acres in Delta Township, Michigan, and includes a worship center, Bible Training Institute, children's center, youth and young adult facilities, Prayer Chapel, Global Prayer Center, Fitness Center, Care facilities, and a medical complex.

Construction of Gilead Healing Center was completed in 2003. This multi-million dollar edifice includes medical facilities, nutritional education, and fitness training. Its most important mission is to equip believers to minister to the sick as Jesus and his disciples did. Medical and osteopathic doctors, doctors of chiropractic and naturopathy, and licensed physical and massage therapists all work harmoniously with trained prayer partners to bring about miraculous healing for sick people from all over the United States.

Under Dave's leadership, 43 daughter and branch churches have been successfully planted in Michigan, the Philippines, Ghana, Ivory Coast, and Zimbabwe. Including all branch and affiliate churches, Mount Hope Churches claim over 20,000 members as of December, 2007.

Dave is founder and president of Mount Hope Bible Training Institute, a fully accredited, church-based leadership institute for training ministers, church planters, and lay people to perform the work of the ministry. Dave also established the Dave Williams' School for Church Planters, located in St. Pete Beach, Florida.

He has authored more than 60 books including best seller, *The New Life...The Start of Something Wonderful* (with over 2 million books sold in eight languages). More recently, he wrote *The World Beyond: The Mysteries of Heaven and How to Get There* (over 100,000 copies sold). His *Miracle Results of Fasting* (Harrison House Publishers) was an Amazon.com five-star top seller for two years in a row.

Dave's articles and reviews have appeared in national magazines such as *Advance*, *Pentecostal Evangel*, *Charisma*, *Ministries Today*, *Lansing Magazine*, *Detroit Free Press*, *World News*, and others.

Dave has appeared on television in the United States and Canada, and has been heard worldwide over *The Hour of Decision*, the weekly radio ministry of the Billy Graham Evangelistic Association. Dave's Sunday messages are available for download at www.mounthopechurch.org.

Along with his wife, Mary Jo, Dave established The Dave and Mary Jo Williams Charitable Mission (Strategic Global Mission), a non-profit ministry providing scholarships to pioneer pastors and ministry students, as well as grants to inner-city children's ministries.

CONTACT INFORMATION

Mount Hope Church and
International Outreach Ministries
202 S. Creyts Road
Lansing, Michigan 48917

For a complete list of Dave Williams'
life-changing books, CDs and videos call:
Phone: 517-321-2780
800-888-7284
TDD: 517-321-8200
or go to our web site:
www.mounthopechurch.org

For prayer requests, call the
Mount Hope Global Prayer Center
24-hour prayer line at:
517-327-PRAY
(517-327-7729)

Must have tools for ministry success

11⁹⁷
PN: IP30086

$10⁹⁷
PN: IP30088

14⁹⁹

Skill for Battle
The Art of Spiritual Warfare

PN: IP30106

10⁹⁷
PN: IP30107

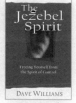

$7⁹⁵
PN: IP30076

9⁹⁵

Elite Prayer Warriors
A Plan for Powerful Intercessory Prayer

PN: IP30105

10⁹⁵
PN: IP30034

$1⁹⁵
PN: IP30003

Shop **decapolisbooks.com** or call 1-800-888-7284